Perfecting Your Watercolours

Ron Ranson's
PAINTING
SCHOOL

Perfecting
Your Watercolours

RON RANSON

ANAYA PUBLISHERS LTD
LONDON

First published in Great Britain in 1995 by
Anaya Publishers Ltd., Strode House,
44-50 Osnaburgh Street, London NW1 3ND.

Editor   Coral Walker
Art Director   Jane Forster
Photographer   Shona Wood
Text   Helen Douglas-Cooper
with Ron Ranson

British Library Cataloguing in Publication Data

Ranson, Ron
    Perfecting Your Watercolours. – (Ron
    Ranson's Painting School Series)
    I. Title II. Series
    751.422

    ISBN 1-85470-211-4

Typeset in Plantin in Great Britain by
Litho Link Ltd, Welshpool, Powys, Wales.
Colour reproduction by HBM Print Pte Ltd, Singapore.
Printed and bound in Malaysia by Times Offset Ltd.

Contents

Introduction

I've probably got one of the most extensive libraries of books on watercolour in the world, and having been through them all I was struck by the fact that every one of them explains how to put down a wash, how to create graduated and variegated washes, how to paint skies or seascapes, and so on, but the one thing they don't tell you is how to design a painting. If you stop to think about it, everything that's made – from cars to cups – is designed, but this whole area is mostly ignored by painting books.

Then I was fortunate to discover the great American watercolour painter and teacher, Ed Whitney, and his mentor, Maitland Graves, also a teacher and the author of *The Art of Color and Design* (published in 1951), who together opened my eyes to the vital role of design in watercolour.

The idea of designing a painting is nothing new – great painters throughout history have incorporated the principles of good design into their work. Look at the work of Turner (1775-1851), John Sell Cotman (1782-1842), Gurtin or David Cox (1783-1859), for example. They only put in what's relevant to the design. Cotman was way ahead of his time in this regard. His paintings are beautifully designed, with interesting, interlocking shapes; every part of the composition is linked to other parts; and it's clear which features are the most important.

Every subject that you decide to paint must be modified in order to produce a good picture. Many amateur painters think that design has nothing to do with painting, so the first thing you've got to realize is that a painting should be designed to be effective.

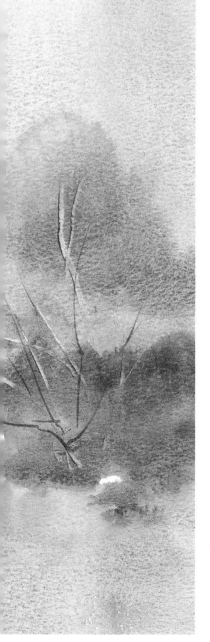

Left, whatever the subject, the elements need to be carefully arranged and balanced to create a unified and interesting painting. Here, the main tree is echoed by the smaller trees around it; vertical lines are balanced by diagonal ones; and the overall cool atmosphere is balanced and intensified by areas of warm colour.

A sense of receding space has been created deliberately by the contrast between sharpness and detail in the foreground and looser forms in the distance, and through the relatively smaller size of things in the distance against those in the foreground.

I am sometimes asked to select the entries in open exhibitions in America. In this situation you're faced with about 300 pictures and you've got to get them down to, for example, 98, because that's all there's room for in the gallery. The first thing I look for is good design, and the first thing I reject is bad design. You don't consider anything else about the paintings to start with, and you probably reject 150 or so because they're badly designed. The artists who painted them hadn't thought about design – they probably thought that if they painted a good tree it would get into the exhibition.

So, if you want to perfect your watercolours, you have to learn to design your paintings. By this, I mean that you need to take the different elements in the subject you are painting and arrange and interpret them in such a way as to create strong, entertaining pictures that hold the viewer's attention. However well you can handle watercolour, you must learn how to manipulate the elements of a painting, such as shape, tone, texture and colour, to create harmony, balance and contrast and to create dominant and unifying features.

It's all right to paint what's in front of you while you are learning to handle the paint, but if you want your work to move into another league, you have to think about design. Whatever you are painting, you need to modify and change it in order to make it a good

Below left, good composition is the basis of a good painting, and here I positioned the main focus of interest, the group of trees, off centre, with lines formed by features such as the reflections and the banks of the river leading to it. The small angular shapes of the rocks in the foreground are balanced by the simple, soft shapes of the distant woods.

Below, expansive space and large shapes are contrasted with the vertical lines of the trees. The shapes coming in from alternate sides of the picture create receding space. Strong shapes in the sky balance those of the land. The cool colour of the mountains in the distance make them recede against the warmer colours of the nearer land. The boat to the left of the picture adds life and a sense of scale to the scene.

picture. Even a simple subject, such as a bowl of flowers, should be placed, not in the dead centre of a picture, but to one side, with something to balance it on the other side.

The most important thing here is to change your attitude and to realize that it's your job as an artist to change things around in order to create a strong, entertaining picture. Unless you do, no amount of technical skill will help you to perfect your work – you'll just keep on painting in the same old way, and you won't progress. Design has rules that anyone can learn, and if we apply them to our own paintings, we can lift them from being technically competent to being full of impact and interest for the viewer.

THE BASICS

The materials described here will help you to work in a design-conscious way. In order to design your paintings, you need to do preliminary tonal sketches, and it's important to do them the right way if they are to help you perfect your watercolours, as they can assist you plan the tonal pattern in a painting in order to create maximum impact. You also need to bear in mind the basics of good composition, deciding on your centre of interest, and arranging the other elements in the picture so that the viewer's attention is led naturally through the scene.

To convey the character of this peaceful woodland scene, I used a combination of large areas of wash, a variety of different types of marks and rough and smooth textures. The composition was planned to lead the eye gradually back through the scene.

Materials

In painting, as in anything else, it is essential to have the right tools for the job, and it's important when you're trying to produce a satisfying watercolour, to have the kind of materials and equipment that will help you to achieve your aim, and that you devise working methods and a working environment that suits you. You will also need a good range of materials for sketching, as well as for painting, if you are to improve the overall standard of your work.

My own views and ideas on this subject are perhaps not entirely conventional, and this is reflected in my choice of materials, especially when it comes to brushes. Most of my brushes are large and flat, which forces me to simplify the subject I'm painting and prevents the dreaded 'fiddling'. I use large tubes of paint, too, and if you can be persuaded to do the same, you'll soon find that you're achieving greater strength of colour and a much wider range of tonal values in your paintings.

BRUSHES

The brush that I use for most of my work is called a hake. It is a broad, flat brush, available in different widths, and is used commonly in Eastern painting. I

The hake, 1in flat and rigger between them can be used to produce a wide range of marks and effects from very soft areas of wash to hard-edged shapes, and from large textural areas to sharp, hard lines.

use the hake in sizes ranging from 3.75–5cm (1½-2in) wide, which at first may seem clumsy and difficult to handle – rather like getting used to a tennis racket with a large head. I promise you, though, that if you persevere with it, you'll soon wonder how you did without it as you learn to cover large areas quickly. You can produce exciting skies, for example, rapidly and boldly – and this will put you in the right mood for the rest of the painting.

People sometimes ask me how I can produce tiny sketches only 5cm (2in) wide with this brush, and the secret is to use only the corner. You can also use just the side of the brush, or even the heel, for other effects. It is worth trying out different ways of using it on scraps of paper, and with practice, you'll soon be using it delicately and in a wide variety of ways for skies, backgrounds, trees, hills and rivers.

Incidentally, this delicacy of touch is vital if you're ever to realize the full potential of the hake. Just because it looks like a house painter's brush, this doesn't mean that it should be used like one!

For man-made objects such as boats, houses and docks, which have sharp, straight edges, I bring the 1in flat into play. Its sharp edge is ideal for producing

Clockwise from bottom left: hake for broad shapes and 1in flat for the sharper shapes; hake and 1in flat; hake used on its side and on the end; hake, 1in flat, and rigger for the fine lines; hake.

13

these hard, more defined surfaces, as well as for distant masts or fence posts. As with the hake, experiment with this brush to see how many different effects you can get by using it in different ways and at different angles. It is also the best brush to use for doing tonal sketches with paint.

My third brush is the rigger. Flexible and long-haired, this is used for calligraphic type work such as tapering branches and foreground grasses.
It's invaluable, too, for adding figures. Try holding it at the very end of the handle for maximum flexibility.

When we look at a subject in nature, at first it appears to be made up of a mass of small random areas of tones and colours, and you have to sort out the main shapes from all this confusion. Large brushes will help you with this, because you have no option but to treat the subject as broad, flat shapes, massing smaller areas together into larger ones, which in turn produces stronger, clearer compositions. I'll talk more about this later, in Tonal Values (page 46) and Shape (page 38).

To make your paintings really interesting, you also need to develop lively, expressive brushmarks. It's

Right, a variety of marks have been made with the hake to create the mixture of shapes and textures in this woodland scene. I added strong colour to the washes in the foreground area.

Below, here I used one sweep of the hake to form the shape of the cat.

possible to use the hake to create a range of different marks, as I've done in the sketches on these pages, from large, smooth expanses of water, to rough ground and textured foliage. And the same applies with the 1in flat. You can also get different effects according to how quickly you move the brush across the paper (the slower the movement, the more paint will be deposited) and at what angle you hold the brush to the paper. It is worth experimenting on some scrap paper to get the feel of using the brushes in different ways and the variety of effects you can create.

Paintings look their most lively and spontaneous when the minimum number of brushstrokes have been used, so think about what effect you want in each place and then go for it boldly and confidently, working as quickly as possible. And resist the temptation to work over an area again, even if it doesn't look quite how you intended. With tricky bits you can make one or two trial runs holding the brush just above the paper so that you know where you want the brushstroke to begin and end; after that make the stroke quickly and with assurance.

Top right, the main shapes were created by bold, sweeping strokes of the hake, combined with the 1in flat for details.

Bottom right, hard-edged and soft shapes contrast with linear marks to create a misty scene with great depth.

PAINT

In order to work freely and create paintings with rich, vibrant areas of colour and strong, rich tones, you need to be uninhibited when you're squeezing out the paint and generous in applying it. I find that a good way to achieve this is to use the large tubes of student-quality paint, which is much cheaper than artist's quality. Try it, using just seven colours (more about these later) as I do. I guarantee that if you're not worrying about the cost of the paint, you'll feel much happier about squeezing out the rich, juicy dollops of paint that are essential for a free and exciting watercolour.

PAPER

Although the expensive hand-made papers are lovely to use, they can be inhibiting because they make you feel that you're wasting good money if you make a mistake. The answer to this is to use a Bockingford 300gsm (140lb) paper, or a paper of equivalent weight. Paper of this weight only buckles slightly when it's wet, and so doesn't need stretching, and with this weight you can work on the back of a discarded painting. Some of the best paintings I've done have been on the backs of other paintings, and I'm sure it's because I felt more relaxed as I didn't feel that I was wasting money.

OTHER EQUIPMENT

Because I paint with big brushes and lots of paint, I like to mix my colours on a large palette. I actually use a white plastic tray, which not only copes well with the hake, but also gives me plenty of room for mixing the paint so that I can see the colours emerging clearly. It's much easier to use a big tray like this than trying to mix colours in the tiny compartments that are common in many palettes, and you can't pick up big scoops of colour from a tiny compartment. The other disadvantage of these palettes is that the paint tends to dry very quickly.

I suppose that one of the most important materials is also the cheapest – a good supply of rags! I couldn't work without them. The hake in particular holds a great deal of water and rags are essential for getting rid of excess water from the brush before applying paint to the paper – this is absolutely vital if you're to get good, rich colour in your paintings.

Keep your equipment simple and ready to use, and you'll always be ready to paint at a moment's notice. A water pot, tubes of paint, brushes, palette and a rag are all you need. Palettes come in a variety of shapes and sizes, including individual dishes for mixing a large quantity of wash, although as an alternative, a big, white, plastic tray gives you lots of room for mixing paints. Hakes are available in a variety of widths, and the wider ones are easier to use than they look.

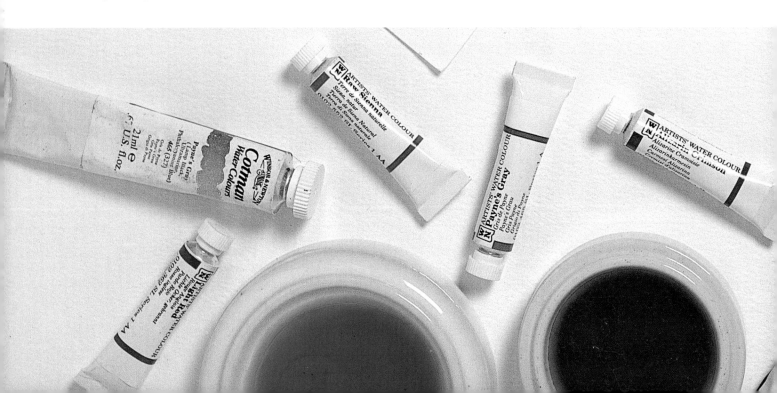

STUDIO SET-UP

You'll find that painting at home is much easier if you can set up a good workspace for yourself, preferably where you don't have to keep clearing everything away. It's important to work on a surface with a slight slope – I use an old draughtsman's table – but if you haven't enough space for a special table, a table-top drawing board is fine and not too difficult to make. I also use a trolley, which holds all my painting equipment. You can move it around if you want to change your working position, and wheel your things out of the way with the minimum of fuss if necessary. In addition, you'll need some storage space for paper and suchlike. After years of making do, I've now got my own purpose-built studio and I admit that I get a thrill each time I walk into it!

DESIGN KIT

In the next section I am going to talk about that essential for a well-organized picture – the tonal sketch. These sketches are what makes the difference between the amateur and the professional, and to do them properly you need just a few more materials.

Tonal sketches involve working with blocks of tone, not line, so you need soft pencils (4B–6B), carpenters' pencils (broad, flat pencils), chalk and charcoal that allow you to get large areas of tone down on paper quickly. You'll also need a soft putty rubber and a sketchpad of ordinary, smooth cartridge paper (not watercolour paper). Once you've assembled your design kit, keep it together and always have it to hand when you go out painting. Hopefully, it will soon become an integral part of your equipment.

A variety of materials can be
used for making tonal sketches
– try them out and see which
you find easiest to use. Here
I've used: top and middle left,
a soft pencil, and immediately
below, charcoal; far left and
bottom, were done with paint.

Tonal sketches

As I have just said, the tonal sketch – or lack of it – is what makes the difference between an amateur and a professional standard of painting. Many people hate doing them, and even among my own students, many have not really understood the full meaning and value of the tonal sketch. So please, do read on. I promise you that if you persevere with these sketches, your painting will soon be in another league altogether.

We're not talking here about line drawings; we are talking about providing ourselves with clear information on the different tones in any scene. The point of this is to work out the tonal value pattern for the scene you are painting – that is, deciding where to place the strongest contrasts, and making sure that lighter tones are played against darker ones in order to make different elements stand out clearly from each other. The tonal values should form a clear and interesting pattern, and the only way you can achieve this is to work it out in a sketch before you put paint to paper.

One other thing: once you've completed your tonal sketch, do follow it while you're painting: match the tones of the colours you put down in each part of the painting to the tones in your sketch. This must sound horribly obvious, but it's all too easy in the excitement of getting out your paints and becoming absorbed in your painting to forget all about tonal values!

You may feel that all this sounds boring and that you just want to plunge straight into the actual painting, but if you really want to perfect your watercolours, you need to work out your design, and you simply can't do this until you've learned how to do a good tonal sketch. Incidentally, you'll save, too, on wasted paint and paper because you'll no longer be producing work that is flat and wishy-washy – because the overall pattern is too weak.

Of course, there are other aspects to creating a good painting, but they all follow on from the good tonal sketch. You start with a strong tonal arrangement and then build up from there. So, those are the reasons for doing the tonal sketch – the 'why', if you like – now let's get down to the 'how'.

First of all, work small (the examples here are about the right size), and try to keep all your tonal sketches to roughly the same size. Next, forget about putting lines around everything and including detail. Instead, concentrate on using blocks of tone to create a strong visual impression. As you look at the scene in front of you in this way, the temptation to do line drawings will quickly disappear. To make it easier, you can break the scene down into three tones – light, medium and dark – and build up the sketch using just these. To do this, use a soft pencil on its side, not its point, or use charcoal or chalk. You create the different tones

This type of sketch, which is just a line drawing, gives you no information at all about the tonal organization or the arrangement of shapes in the scene.

A simple sketch like this, using just three tones, will help you see the main shapes and tonal areas of your composition clearly.

by applying different pressures. For the lightest tones you'll need to use gentle pressure (about 10g/½oz), while to get a strong, dark tone, you'll need to use heavy pressure (about 450g/1lb).

Forget about details such as doors or windows in buildings, or blades of grass, and concentrate on the main shapes. Now look at your sketch as a pattern and ask yourself if what you've got is clear and interesting. If not, try again – I often do – perhaps adjusting the values around the centre of interest to create more contrast. Eventually you'll find that a tonal sketch only takes about five minutes, and you'll certainly know after only a minute or two whether you've got something acceptable or not. Just five minutes – and I make no apology for repeating this – will make all the difference in the world to your painting.

Sketches like these will give you confidence when beginning a painting. Although done with different media – pencil, charcoal and paint – they all break the scene down into blocks of a few tones. You can then check the balance of tones and shapes before you start painting in earnest.

Top, the man is set against the light areas on the ground, and balanced by the dark group of trees.

Middle, the windswept tree is balanced by the fence posts on the right and echoed by the cloud.

Bottom, the eye is drawn through the foreground to the dark figure, and on to the light building behind.

In all these sketches, the main elements are differentiated from each other through the use of varied tones, and you can see that the final painting will be balanced and interesting.

Composition

Before we go into the details of designing a picture, let's look at what makes for good and bad basic composition – the things on which judges of competitions actually assess your work – because a strong basic composition is vital to creating an interesting painting.

Composition is the process of arranging the basic subject of your painting. In order to create a good composition you need to manipulate the subject and move things around in such a way that you focus the viewer's attention on the centre of interest and prevent the eye being led out of the picture.

When we first start to paint, we just want to put down exactly what is in front of us. We simply don't think about re-arranging it, and so the same faults crop up time and time again – lines that lead out of the picture, figures, or strong tonal contrasts, placed right at the edge of the picture, no centre of interest and so on – simply because the overall composition hasn't been thought through.

Now, however, we're looking to perfect our work, and to do this we must start to re-arrange elements in the picture. You need to focus on the most interesting feature in your subject and manipulate everything else to support that main feature.

THE CENTRE OF INTEREST
The first thing you have to decide on is the centre of interest in your painting. Everyone wants to paint a beautiful piece of scenery, but even when you've found that perfect little stream and tree, you must be sure to have a dominant feature. When painting a

In many scenes there simply isn't an obvious centre of interest, you have to create it. Here, I had two options. In the picture on the left, I decided to emphasize the boat moving across the water, so lightened it in tone against the background and reduced the tonal contrast on the left of the picture. I also reduced the amount of foreground to bring the boat closer. In the version on the right, I went for the silhouette of the church and surrounding buildings, and to draw attention to them I darkened the buildings and set them against a light sky, playing down the tonal contrast on the right so that the boat blended in with the background.

woodland scene, always make one tree larger than the others, even if in fact they're all the same size. Remember that it is not enough simply to copy nature, we must rearrange it to create an harmonious painting full of excitement and vitality. If there are two strong features in your scene, you have to be ruthless and subdue one of them because you can't have two centres of interest in one scene.

It is a good idea to put down on paper what constitutes the scene you want to paint. This will help you to be clear in your own mind why you are doing the painting, and it will also help you to stick to your original idea. Ask yourself: What am I painting this for? What really interests me about the subject? Is it the subject itself, or is it the weather or lighting conditions. When you've done all this you may find that the scene you want to paint doesn't have a focal point. If this is the case then it's up to you to create one. It may be that the subject is secondary to the atmosphere. You might choose a subject that is not in itself picturesque, like a bonfire, because of the way the light from the fire is catching someone's profile, or the way the smoke curls up towards the sky.

Once you have decided what you want to convey about your subject, you'll find it much easier to plan the composition and to make other decisions, for example about your choice of colours. If you want to convey a cold, grey morning, you'll know that you need to use predominantly cool, grey colours; for a warm, sunny atmosphere you'll use predominantly warm colours (I'll say more about this in the section on Colour starting on page 66).

POSITIONING

Once you are clear about your centre of interest, you next need to decide where to position it, and there are certain places in the painting where it simply won't work. It should never be in the centre of the painting, or right at the edge, nor in a corner. Ideally, the centre of interest should be placed at a different distance from each side.

There are various ways of drawing the viewer's attention to the centre of interest. You can place the

PRACTICE

Try a series of paintings of the same scene or subject, changing your viewpoint for each one. Approach it from each side; if there is high ground nearby, try looking down on the subject; and try getting as low as you can and looking up. Compare the results and see which effect you like best. You'll notice that a change in viewpoint can alter the relative importance of features in the scene. If you are looking down on it, everything will seem smaller and less significant, whereas if you are looking up, any tall features will tower over you, and this can play an important part in the emotional impact of the painting. If you are looking up at the subject, this may also give you the opportunity to create visual impact by emphasizing silhouettes. If you paint the same scene at different times of the day, you can also make use of changing shadows.

You could try a similar series of paintings in which you change the focus of interest in each one. Choose a landscape that has two or three interesting features and use contrasts in tone, colour and shape to make a different feature the centre of interest in each one.

Far left, in this scene I've used a colour contrast of red against green to draw attention to the building, which is the focus of interest.

Left, here the large, strong shapes of the bridge, compared to those in other parts of the scene, immediately draw your attention. The tonal contrast is also greater around the bridge than in the foreground and distance.

Right, I've made use of a strong tonal contrast to draw the viewer's eye to the little boat house. There is also a strong contrast in shape here, the boat house being a hard, angular shape against the softer, rounded shapes in other parts of the painting.

The eye is led in to the scene by the road. Notice how the sides of the road lead in from two adjacent sides of the painting. The row of posts and the contours of the hills also converge on the building.

strongest tonal contrast — the lightest light against the darkest dark – around the centre of interest. You could use the brightest colours there, or more detail than in other parts of the painting. Thinking of shapes, you could make one larger than other similar shapes. However, the most powerful and visually exciting of all the devices that you can use to emphasize the focal point is tonal contrast. This always draws the viewer's attention, and will dominate other effects in the painting.

CHOICE OF VIEWPOINT

Having chosen our subject, we often have a choice of viewpoints from where we can paint. When selecting the viewpoint, one of the main things you have to decide is where to place the horizon in the painting – do you want it high or low in the picture? If it is high, you can cut out a lot of sky – maybe almost all of it, but don't cut it out completely because it is the source of light and mood in the scene. A high horizon can

create quite a claustrophobic, enclosed atmosphere. A low horizon, on the other hand, will place the emphasis on the sky. You can place it very low and make the sky the subject of the painting, which is well worth doing when the sky is dramatic. If you have time, walk around and look at your subject from different directions before choosing a position from which to paint.

LEAD-INS FOR THE EYE

Various devices can be used to lead the eye to the focal point. Converging lines formed by fences, roadsides, the skyline and so on, can meet at that spot. Or you could have curving lines or shapes, such as a winding road or river, leading to it. Make sure, though, that a road or river intended to lead in, doesn't accidentally lead out. If it leads in at an oblique angle to the bottom of the picture, it will have the effect of leading the eye away. Instead, make sure it enters at right angles to the edges of the picture ie, across a corner.

Above, the S-shape road leads through the foreground to the focus of interest. The brightest touch of colour, together with a strong tonal contrast, also draw the eye to the building. Interest continues up into the sky, and the attention is brought back into the scene by the large tree on the left.

Left, the river leads in and the lines of the hills on either side of the bridge lead down to it.

CREATING DEPTH

Think of the picture in terms of foreground, middle ground and distance. The foreground must not compete with the focal point in terms of detail, contrast, strength of colour and so on. What it should do is to provide the lead-in to the main area of interest, and the eye should be able to move on from there to explore other areas, before being led back to the focal point. I'm sure you've often seen, as I have, pictures with something like a wall or fence across the foreground, forming a visual barrier and preventing the eye from moving further into the picture.

Forms in the foreground, middle ground and distance, should overlap each other in order to link together different areas of the painting. A sense of depth is created in this way as one element appears in front of or behind another. This overlapping also helps to hold the composition together, because if elements in different parts of the scene stand in isolation from each other, the resulting picture will look disjointed as well as flat.

Another way to increase the sense of space is to make the edges between one object and another more indistinct in the distance than in the foreground. The

Left, tonal contrast, texture, detail and colour have all been reduced in the background.

Right, a sense of depth is achieved through setting the large foreground building against the very small shapes of the distant buildings.

Left, here I've used texture, detail and bright splashes of colour in the foreground, gradually reducing the amount of each in the middle ground and distance.

size of the main shapes should be logical in relation to each other; ie, larger shapes appear nearer than smaller ones. Colour is stronger in the foreground, and duller and cooler in the distance. Texture and detail should normally be more apparent in the foreground and not visible in the distance, so be careful not to include them in the distance just because you know they are there.

You need to think about all these things when you are planning the basic composition, and here again, your tonal sketch will help you to establish the best composition, as well as clarifying the tonal organization. You'll need to be able to see whether the main shapes balance each other, whether your strongest tonal contrast occurs around the centre of interest – rather than some other part of the painting where it will distract the viewer's attention – and whether you have created a sense of distance by the use of tones and shapes.

Group objects like trees or boats together rather than stringing them out across the picture. Don't be afraid to move things around, or to add in or leave out elements if this will improve the composition.

PRACTICE
To help you create a sense of depth in a scene, try a painting in which the tonal values, intensity of colour and degree of detail decreases as the scene recedes away into the distance, making the changes as gradual as you can. Then do a second painting, trying to get an even more gradual reduction on tonal contrasts and colour changes. To do this, begin with the lightest possible washes, and increase the tonal values, strength of colour and amount and fineness of detail step by step as you work forwards, aiming to end up really exaggerating the foreground. This may give you something that is too extreme in contrast, but this is just an exercise and you can tone down the contrasts again in the next painting. The point is to encourage you to experiment, so that you can judge the relative effects of colours and tonal values against each other and really begin to feel that you have some control over the tones and colours in your work.

Left, this scene is clearly divided into three planes: the foreground, with warm colours, strong tones and detail; the middle distance, with a cooler colour and less detail on the tree-covered spur jutting into the lake; and the distance, where the colour is cooler and the tonal values are weaker.

Right the eye is led through the foreground by the alternating lights and darks to the building. The suggestion of a path on the hillside behind leads the attention on. I created a feeling of space through strong colour and fine detail in the foreground, and duller cooler, colour in the distance.

PARTS OF
A PAINTING

In order to design your paintings well, you have to see your subject in a new way. Line, shape, tonal value, texture and colour are the components that you have to work with, and you need to analyze the subjects of your paintings in these terms, learning to arrange and vary lines and shapes, creating interesting tonal patterns and different textures, and using colour to introduce interest and atmosphere.

Lines and shapes, tonal contrast, rough and soft textures, and colour are all used in this winter scene to convey the mood of a cold but bright day with snow blanketing the ground. The sharply delineated trees and grasses in the foreground contrast with the soft, barely distinguishable, shapes of the trees in the distant wood.

Line

The first aspect that you may need to change in your search for perfecting your painting, is the way you think about line in a scene. Perhaps you haven't thought too much about this in the past, but think about it now. Next time you're sitting in front of your chosen scene, look at the lines that are apparent in the different elements. Ask yourself what types of line are there, in what direction do they run, and whether there's more of one than another. You'll soon see the lines created by masts, posts, trees, steps, even shadows on the profile of a building. Then ask yourself how you can alter or add to them in order to create a stronger composition.

Bear in mind, also, that when we talk about line in a scene, this does not just mean things that look like a line, such as stalks of grass, or rigging on boats. It can also include the edges of solid objects like doors and windows, steps, the lines of the roofs of buildings, and so on. It can also include broad lines, or long, thin shapes, such as extended shadows across the ground.

There are two kinds of line, straight and curved: decide which one suits your composition best.

DIRECTION
As well as the type of line, you need to be aware of the direction of any lines in your painting. Lines are either horizontal, vertical or oblique. You should include all three, but one should be dominant. If the scene contains mainly horizontal lines, you should include a few verticals, even if you have to alter one or two features to provide them.

The grasses in the foreground form mainly curving lines, and I used the straight lines created by branches in the tree and the line of hills in the distance to contrast with them. The strong diagonal emphasis evokes a windswept atmosphere, set off by the horizontals on the shores of the lake.

FORMAT

The two formats you'll usually want to use for outdoor scenes are landscape, or horizontal, and upright, although I find that the landscape format is usually best for landscape scenes. You should decide which to use based on the main shape and direction of the subject. If the main subject is tall and thin, or has a strong vertical thrust, it will suit an upright format best. If the subject is broader than it is tall, has a wide horizon, or a strong horizontal thrust, it will fit best into a landscape format.

You should consider very carefully the characteristics of each subject and the overall impression you want to create before deciding which format is best to use.

PRACTICE

Try doing a few very quick sketches in pencil or paint of different scenes showing the various types and directions of lines you can see. Remember that we're not talking about outlines, but the lines evident in the different features that you are including in the picture.

You do not need to draw in the actual features themselves – these sketches can in fact be quite abstract. The point is to help you spot the linear elements in a scene quickly.

Buildings, steps, and even people, can provide strong linear elements in a scene even though the lines are not – in the case of buildings, for example – actual lines, but edges. Here, the mainly vertical direction of the linear elements in the composition, formed by the edges of the buildings, lines of the roofs, shutters, chimneys and people, is contrasted with the prominent diagonal of the railings on the side of the building.

PRACTICE

There are various ways of introducing types and directions of lines into a scene if it needs them. Horizontal lines can be created by fallen trees, branches, horizontals in buildings, verges and riverbanks; oblique lines can be created with lines on the ground, paths, and so on, or by tipping uprights such as grasses and fence posts so that they are at an angle.

Analyze some of your old paintings in terms of line and think about ways in which you could introduce more linear elements or emphasize the ones that are there. Ask yourself: do they include straight and curved lines? Could you include more of one or the other? And do the paintings have an overall sense of direction? Make sketches or do new versions of the paintings to try out different possibilities.

Try some sketches analysing the linear elements in a scene, and think about which ones to emphasize to make a strong painting.

Your choice of format should be dictated by the subject. The horizontal emphasis of the composition on the left and the wide horizon suggest a landscape format, while the tall, vertical thrust of the trees and their reflections (below left) is emphasized by a vertical format.

Although the painting below doesn't contain many lines as such, it has a strong diagonal linear emphasis created by the course of the stream, the lie of the rocks and the overhanging trees. The sharp changes of direction in the stream convey a rapid sense of movement as the water rushes down over the rocks.

Shape

As I've said before, when we start painting, we see the subjects as they are – buildings, boats, trees, mountains, and so on. However, to progress, we have to learn to see these features as shapes. We have to become aware of the size and scale of each shape, and how all the different shapes fit together.

Ask yourself which is the largest shape and which is the smallest? Do these shapes butt up next to each other or do some overlap others? Are any of the shapes you see repeated?

There are three types of shape: angular, curved and rectangular, and the different subjects in a scene will fit into one of these. Although two or all three types of shape may be present in your painting, only one should dominate.

SHAPES TO AVOID

Some shapes are very boring – namely, the circle, the square and triangles with two or three equal sides. The reason we find them boring is because they lack variety. The square has all four sides the same length. In the circle, all points on the circumference are an equal distance from the centre. And a triangle is dull if two or more of its sides and angles are the same, even if this is disguised by the fact that it is lying on its side.

In order to create an eye-catching painting, the shapes need to be made interesting, even if this means altering the shapes of the things that you see. A squarish shape can be changed by making some of its sides longer than the others –I'm talking here about the main shapes in the composition, not details such as

Above, although you should include different types of shapes in a painting, one must dominate. Here, square shapes are dominant. From the sketch (right) you can see that the underlying pattern is clearly made up of mainly squarish shapes, although they are varied to maintain interest.

Left, this painting contains the three basic shapes – the group of buildings, which I've made rectangular rather than square; the boat, which is triangular, but I've broken up its outline; and the trees behind the boat, which I've made curved rather than circular. It's important to develop the habit of seeing the objects in your pictures in terms of these underlying basic shapes.

PRACTICE

Choose a subject – one where the objects have an obvious shape, such as boats, or buildings and trees against the sky. Begin by painting the negative shapes, ie the spaces around the main objects, as flat shapes. Remember that negative and positive shapes must interlock, so include or create incidents around the edges and adjust the shapes themselves if necessary. If you want to, you can then develop the painting further, but the point of the exercise is to become aware of the negative shapes in a scene and to regard them as being as important as the positive ones.

This painting includes all types of shapes, but each is varied in outline and in size. Triangles occur in the boats, the church spire, and in some of the roofs; squarish shapes in the buildings and boats that are sideways on; the trees and clouds form roughly circular shapes. It's important not to forget about the sky when you're judging the balance of the shapes in a composition.

The sketch above shows how smaller shapes should be massed together into larger ones that interlock across the whole painting.

windows. Another example might be a tree where the foliage roughly fits into a circle. This will be much more interesting if you change it into an irregular curved shape. A triangular shape can be altered by changing the length of a side or the size of an angle.

It is easy to paint a square building, or a triangular mountain, without realizing that it fits into one of these shapes, but with a little thought and practice you'll soon develop the ability to recognize the underlying shapes of the objects you are painting.

INTERESTING SHAPES
In addition to altering shapes that are dull, there are other qualities that make shapes interesting. Make sure that a shape has two dimensions; that is, that it is wider than it is high, or vice versa. Give the shape direction by slanting it in a particular direction. And remember that the direction should fit the overall composition, not point away from the centre of interest or out of the painting.

Also, shapes should have 'incidents' around their edges. This may sound complicated, but all it means is that all around the edge of a shape, little bits should protrude into whatever is next to it, and vice versa, so that shapes fit together like the pieces of a jigsaw puzzle. The size and direction of these incidents should be varied, as should the space between them.

Finally, no two shapes should be the same size, so you need to adjust them so that they vary. You can also use size to give emphasis to one feature over another.

PRACTICE

Take a scene and break it down into the main shapes. To do this, paint it using a limited number of colours – they needn't be realistic – or even use one colour in a few tones from light to dark, and use just a large brush as this will prevent you fiddling with smaller areas. To make the exercise easier, choose a subject with strong, simple, clear shapes. If you look at the scene through screwed up eyes, this will help you to see it in terms of large areas. Try to see shadows as shapes in their own right, and where shadow falls across different objects, treat it as one continuous shape. If your first attempt at this doesn't look very good, don't worry. You may need to make a few attempts to get the hang of it. Then you can start to adjust the shapes in order to create a strong pattern, and you'll feel much more in control of your subject.

Left, this consists mainly of squarish shapes, but I've made them rectangular rather than exact squares.

Top right, circular shapes in the sky are echoed by the bend in the estuary. The edges of the clouds are very soft and diffuse, creating interest and blending them into the overall sky area. The outline of the breakwater is broken by posts. I've balanced the large, soft sky area with the small, angular, sharply defined shape of the boat.

Middle, strong triangular shapes are varied from building to building, and these are balanced by the square shapes and rounded forms of the trees.

Bottom, all the shapes here have interesting outlines, with incidents around their edges that help interlock the positive and negative shapes.

POSITIVE AND NEGATIVE SHAPES

People often don't think about the negative shapes in their paintings, only the positive ones; the positive shapes being the actual objects – houses, trees, people and so on – and the negative those formed by the spaces around and between the objects. The thing to watch out for is that the boring shapes can crop up as negative as well as positive. Remember – negative shapes should have the same qualities as positive ones. They should be interesting and have direction and incidents round the edges, although of course this will happen anyway if the positive shapes are interesting.

When using watercolour, you need to be especially aware of negative shapes, because of the need to leave the paper white – perhaps it's helpful to think of it as saving and shaping the white areas.

PRACTICE

Look through your old paintings and find one where you think the shapes could be altered to make them more interesting. This could apply particularly where you have several boats or mountains in a scene, which might appear as regular triangular shapes, or buildings, which have been portrayed as a series of too-similar rectangular shapes. Re-paint the scene, concentrating on altering the shapes in order to make them interesting, and remember to create incidents around the edges of things so that all the shapes in the scene interlock.

The strong, dark negative shapes of the foliage behind the castle, the shadow in the gateway and the foreground foliage have been used to define the main subject, the castle walls. The walls themselves have been put in very simply with a light wash or left as white paper.

Right, the strong curves of the main subject and its reflection create interesting negative shapes all around. It is also balanced by larger, unobtrusive areas of straight edges and rectangular shapes. The tree on the left and its reflection are also important in balancing and unifying the composition.

Tonal values

When we talk about tonal values we simply mean the lightness or darkness of an area or object irrespective of its colour. For example, if you have a red roof against green trees, although they are different colours, their tone is the same.

Tonal values can be thought of as a grey scale, maybe from 1, representing black, to 10, representing white, and you need to utilize the whole range from dark to light if you are to improve your paintings, imbuing them with excitement and sparkle.

Many students keep tonal values too close to each other. They seem to be afraid of the rich darks and the white of the paper. The temptation is to stay in the middle range because it's a nice, safe little comfort zone, but just think how boring it would be to hear a piano played only in the middle of its range.

Thinking again in terms of the scale 1–10, you'll see many paintings at around 5–7. They're totally lacking in interest and avoid the use of dark against light and light against dark, which is always the most exciting part of a painting. By using the whole range of tones all the way from 1 to 10, you are now going to avoid boring yourself and your viewers.

COLOUR AND TONAL VALUE

A picture should be made up of lights and darks in areas of greatest interest, with mid-tones in the supporting areas and background. This kind of tonal organization will give a painting an overall sense of design. In order to achieve this, you need to be able to identify the tonal value of different colours, so that you can translate the tones you need into colour.

Each colour has a 'natural' tonal value, which is the value of that colour straight from the tube. Most colours fall in the middle of the tonal range, except for yellow and orange, which are light, and violet, which is dark. You lighten a colour by adding water, and darken a colour by adding blue, Paynes grey, or a little of its complementary colour.

SIMPLIFICATION OF TONES

Any scene is made up of dozens of different tones from white to black and you need to be able to simplify them, or mass them together. Look at your subjects with your eyes screwed up as this will cut out details and help you see the different tonal areas more easily.

In this painting it is easy to see how I've followed the tonal sketch by making the tonal values of the colours I used in the painting to those in the sketch, the result being that the painting has the same clear tonal organization and a strong sense of recession. I used mid-toned, warm bright colours in the foreground, and the eye is drawn through them to the point of strongest tonal contrast in the middle ground, the tonal contrast being reduced in the distance.

See shape and tonal value together, because shapes are composed of tonal value.

Look for places where you can eliminate the boundaries between shapes by letting adjacent dark areas merge, and the same for adjacent light and mid-toned areas. By grouping small shapes into larger ones, you will create a more unified picture.

To prevent the picture looking flat and dull, plan the main areas of light, dark and mid tones, and when you paint, work variations in tone into each one. Screw up your eyes again when looking at your painting. If areas that should be distinct have a tendency to merge together, increase the tonal contrast between them.

DEVELOPING A VALUE PATTERN

Plan the tonal arrangement before you start. This is where the tonal sketch is so important. Having done your tonal sketch, refer to it while you paint – there's no point in planning the painting if you then don't carry out the plan – and if you don't plan it you're back to square one!

Study the subject, looking at the different shapes and how they could be massed together into tones.

These two pictures provide a clear example of the importance of using a wide range of tones. The one above, in which light and mid tones were used, is flat and dull. The one on the right, on the other hand, has a strong impact, depth, and a sense of movement and sparkling light through the use of the widest possible range of lights and darks.

Also decide where you want the strongest tonal contrast, ie, around the centre of interest, and adjust the tones to reduce the contrast between them in other areas of the painting.

Look at your tonal sketch in terms of a pattern: ask yourself whether the blocks of tone make an interesting pattern. Remember – the tonal pattern is the foundation of your painting. Train yourself to see a picture in terms of pattern, not only in terms of trees and houses. Some scenes may look rather flat, but it is your job as an artist to intensify what you see. Don't be afraid to employ strong darks and brilliant lights. They create interest and vibrancy more than any other aspect of a painting.

If a value pattern isn't apparent to start with, begin sketching anyway and look for ways of creating a pattern by exaggerating the tones that you see. Try variations on your first attempt, altering the lights and darks until you have a pleasing effect.

One of the best ways to find out if you're getting a good range of tones is to photocopy your paintings. If the photocopy is flat and boring, you know that there is not enough difference between the tonal values you have used. Also try reducing the size of the picture when you photocopy it. I tried this with a few of mine, and was delighted when some came out just as clear as the original. Aim to be able to reduce them to the size of a postage stamp and still get clear results.

Left, in this version of the scene I've introduced several gradations of tone between light and dark in order to clarify features in the scene and add interest. Try to think in terms of giving each area one basic tone, and then work variations into it.

If you're confused by the large number of different tonal values you can see in a scene, begin by painting it in about seven tones, as I've done above, massing close tones together into larger shapes. If you look again at the first painting on the left, you'll see how you can introduce slight variations of tone into each area while still retaining the basic structure of larger shapes.

Here, I developed areas of a light tonal value across the buildings and boats, with small touches of dark tones provided by the figures and the shadow around the window. The composition is unified by mid-tones through the sky, distance and foreground. This tonal sketch worked as an interesting and balanced pattern in its own right, so the painting worked out well too.

PRACTICE

Make a grey scale, with 10 equal steps from white to black. You can use soft pencil, charcoal, or black and white paint for this. Then take each of your colours in turn and make a light to dark scale with it, trying to match each step to the tones on the grey scale. Darken your colours using a darker-toned but similar colour, or use a complementary colour.

In this painting, I created an area of dark tonal value through the tree and across the foreground, set against the small, light-toned area around the boat, with mid-tones occupying the largest area in the composition. To look interesting, varying tonal values should occupy different sized areas of the composition in this way.

This version is too symmetrical – and therefore dull – because the light and mid-toned areas are a similar size, and the two dark shapes are too evenly balanced.

The larger light shape balances the small dark one, but they are both isolated, whereas in the main picture the dark areas in the two features link up visually.

Left and right, in this scene, I tried several different ways of creating a value pattern. The one I finally chose to paint was with light-toned buildings set against dark trees, balanced by a dark tree on the right.

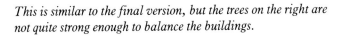

This is similar to the final version, but the trees on the right are not quite strong enough to balance the buildings.

Here, the two light areas are competing with each other. They are linked by the band of dark tone, but they need to be varied in size and tone.

AERIAL PERSPECTIVE

Aerial perspective is the term we use to describe the effect that we can see when we look into the distance, where things become hazy and indistinct as they recede into the horizon. This effect is due to particles of moisture and dust in the atmosphere, which progressively veil the scene. As a result, darker tones become progressively lighter and light tones become slightly darker, ie, they draw closer together – and remember that this tonal recession occurs in the sky as well – so that at the horizon there is very little variation in tonal value as land and sky blends into each other.

Aerial perspective also affects colours. It reduces the brightness, or saturation, of colours, so that they become progressively duller towards the horizon. The atmosphere also tends to filter out yellow, so colours become cooler and bluer the further away they are. Detail and texture are also progressively reduced the greater the distance they are away from you.

If you want to create a convincing impression of depth and space in your paintings, the effects of aerial perspective are something that you need to employ or even exaggerate. Warm colours, strong tonal contrasts, details and textural effects should appear in the foregrounds of your paintings, but you should reduce these effects as the scene recedes, so that colours become cooler and duller, tones become paler and closer, and details and textures disappear. The general effect near the horizon should be indistinct.

Above, the strongest contrast between light and dark has been placed in the foreground, and the contrast has been gradually reduced back through the scene, creating a strong sense of depth. Notice that the sky has been treated in the same way.

Left, in this colour example of aerial perspective, the tonal values and the strength of the colours have both been reduced back through the scene.

PRACTICE

Take one colour and produce the greatest number of steps from light to dark that you can, so that you get to know its potential.

Make a monochrome painting of a scene using just five or seven tones. French ultramarine or burnt umber are good colours to use, and work small. Use the white of the paper for the highlights, and to get the darkest tone use the paint with almost no water. Practice this and try to reach the point where you can get the correct tone for each area first time off. Work on scraps of paper and use a 1in flat brush as this will prevent you fiddling with any details.

Texture

Texture is the surface quality of whatever you are painting – rocks are hard and rough, clouds are soft. These qualities can be recreated through the way you handle the paint, to add variety and interest to a painting. Some students ignore texture altogether, working with the same amount of water all the way through a picture. This type of painting is rather like having a whole orchestra composed of fiddles with nothing exciting to create a contrast. A picture should always be entertaining, and one of the ways to achieve this is to make use of different textures, so that it is like a full orchestra with trumpets, violins, timpani and so on, producing a glorious amalgam of sound.

Texture can play a large part in capturing the mood of a scene, too, whether it's a misty morning, or a raging sea in a storm.

Any painting should have a range of textures, but one texture should dominate. If you are painting a misty scene, you will probably paint the background wet into wet. A good contrast to this would be to introduce a hard rock into the foreground, which would emphasize the soft, misty effect of the overall scene. Rocks are perhaps best done with a dry brush technique – more of that later.

As a watercolourist, you've got more chance to create different textures than anyone else.

Watercolour probably has more potential in this way than any other medium, and not many people explore it fully. However, it's yet another technique that, once learned, will vastly improve your painting and help you to achieve sparkling, professional results.

TYPES OF TEXTURE

There are three different types of texture – rough, smooth and soft. In watercolour, the textures can be varied by changing the amount of water you use with the paint. Good textural differences can be obtained, too, by working on either dry or wet paper to create hard or soft edges.

Watercolour provides the opportunity to produce a wide range of textures. Some of them are created in a quite unorthodox way. Below left: top, the paint was applied using paper; right, a credit card was pressed into a damp wash to remove some of the colour; left, thick paint was added into a wet wash to produce more intense areas of colour; bottom, a combination of textures. Below: top, a smooth, hard edge was created using a 1 in flat brush; right, a combination of dry brush and wet into wet; left, a wet wash was applied to damp paper, causing the colour to spread widely; bottom, the paint was applied with clingfilm (plastic wrap).

Right, the soft texture of the clouds and water, with colour diffused gently through these areas, is set against the hard, rough texture of the headland. Notice how I have introduced touches of different texture into each, however; the headland has soft, diffused shadow areas, and there are hard-edged areas in the water and sky. I created the effect of light on the water by sweeping a dryish brush across dry paper.

Above, I used wet-into-wet washes to create the very soft, diffused impression of trees in the background, and in the foreground area. Against these I set the hard shape of the building, which I painted on dry paper along with the lines of the fence.

Right, in this scene I created the bright touches of colour in the foreground by working neat paint into an area of wash that is still wet so that the colour diffuses around the edges but does not spread and lose its strength. The hard outline of the hill contrasts sharply with the soft foliage.

For a soft, smooth, texture, work on wet paper. If you use a wet brush on wet paper, you will get a very diffuse, uncontrollable result. So it's best to use a dry brush on wet paper, which will give you a lovely, soft but controllable effect.

For a hard, smooth texture, use a loaded brush on dry paper. And for a rough texture, used a dry brush loaded with plenty of paint – but not diluted with water – and drag it quickly across the paper surface to create a broken, scumbled effect.

EDGES

I'm sure you have already noticed that the quality of the edges around areas of paint can vary from hard and sharp to soft and diffused, or fading away to nothing, and this is another feature that we can manipulate to our advantage. Basically, to create a hard edge you need to apply the paint to dry paper, and to create a soft edge you should apply it to damp paper – the damper the paper, the softer and more diffused the edges will be.

The type of edge you give different areas in the painting is important for two reasons. First, it is important that each object has the correct type and texture of edge, or silhouette, for what it is, in order to make it recognizable. For instance, a rock, a building, the sails of a boat, and so on, should have hard edges, while a bush, areas of cloud, smoke, mist and so on should have mainly soft edges, although, as with everything else, there should always be a little of both. For example, while clouds would be predominantly soft, a few hard edges here and there will add interest to your sky.

The second point about edges is that if something is painted with a mainly hard edge, this will separate it from what is behind it in the painting, suggesting space between the two, while something that is painted with a mainly soft edge will blend in with whatever is behind it, giving the impression that the two are touching.

Above, I've indicated the rough, hard texture of the rocks because they are seen close up. The land in the distance is treated softly, as is the foreground, which throws the rocks into sharp relief. The figure is quite sharply defined to draw attention to it. I created the spray against the rocks with a sharp blade.

Left, the features in this scene – buildings, crates and boats – are solid objects, and I've given them hard edges, although in places I've let the outline fade or blend into neighbouring areas so that they don't stand as isolated objects.

Left, the mountains and foreground rocks have hard edges, because this is their nature. The clouds, in contrast, have mainly soft edges, because they are soft and vaporous, although I've introduced a few hard edges here and there.

Right, buildings are solid, so I've painted them with hard edges, whereas the softness of the foliage is conveyed by rounded shapes and soft, broken edges.

PRACTICE

Sometimes we need to experiment with our paints on scraps of paper in order to find out how to control the paint and how to create different effects, and this applies particularly to texture.

To make very soft, diffused effects, for instance for clouds, mist, or distant parts of a scene, apply a wash to wet paper. For stronger colour effects that are still soft, apply only slightly diluted paint to wet paper – dampened either with water or with a wash you have already put down – and mop the brush on a damp rag or sponge first to remove any excess water. The drier your brush when you apply the paint, the less the colour will spread.

For a hard, smooth texture, try applying a wash to dry paper, and for a hard, rough texture, apply paint on a dry brush to dry paper, dragging it across to create a broken, scumbled effect.

There are many other ways of applying paint that can produce interesting and unusual textural effects. You can apply it with a sponge, which creates a broken, mottled effect, or with scrunched-up cling film, which produces a harder-edged result than a sponge. Another way is to apply paint with a piece of paper rather than a paintbrush.

Right, the hard-edged silhouette of the buildings helps explain what the shapes are, and also makes them stand out from the sky behind.

Above, true to their characters, the solid shapes of the hills have hard edges, while the clouds have soft edges, although there are touches of the opposite in each.

Left, I've painted the nearer features in the scene with harder edges, while things further away are softer, so that they blend into the background.

Colour

The best way to learn about colour is to use just a few. Many people make the mistake of using far too many, squeezing out a ready-made colour for every hue that they think they may need.

Buying lots of ready-made colours can be expensive, as you'll never need all of them in any one painting. The other drawback to using a large number of tube paints is that you never really get to know the colours you are using. A few colours will become like close friends, giving you the chance to learn and appreciate the full potential of each one.

I use just seven colours in my palette – lemon yellow, raw sienna, light red, alizarin crimson, burnt umber, ultramarine blue and Paynes grey – and I suggest you do the same. You can mix a wide range of colours, tints and tones from these seven, and with

time and practice you should reach the stage where you know your colours well enough to mix a rich purple, ochry brown or a grey-green without even having to think about it.

QUALITIES OF COLOUR

I'm not going to show you here how to mix each colour you'll need – that will come with practice – but how to use colours to create lively, interesting and atmospheric paintings. To do that, we first need to look at the different qualities of colours – this is very important, so please bear with me.

Each colour has three properties, known as its hue, tonal value and chroma. Hue is the term we use to distinguish one colour from another – red, yellow, blue and so on. Tonal value is the lightness or

A scale from dark to light in red. The lightest tone was created by adding a lot of water, and the darkest by adding very little.

The same red, bright to dull. These two scales show that the tonal value of a colour is not the same as its brightness or dullness.

Ultramarine blue ranging from dark to light.

Ultramarine blue from fully saturated to dull.

Left, this scene has a broad range of tones from light to dark, and also areas of dull and bright colour. The touches of bright colour are small, in contrast to larger areas of dull colour, and provide focus.

The colour wheel, consisting of the three primaries: red, yellow and blue; in between are the three secondaries mixed from them: orange, green and purple. The wheel can be expanded by adding in the intermediate colours: green-yellow, blue-green, purple-blue, red-purple and so on, between the primaries and secondaries.

darkness of a colour measured against a scale from white to black, and we had a look at this in the previous chapter. Chroma refers to the brightness or dullness of a colour. You will also sometimes come across chroma described as colour strength or colour saturation. Another thing to bear in mind in relation to chroma is that as a colour becomes less bright it also becomes more grey.

If we can manipulate these aspects of colour, we can use colours to create specific effects of space, light, modelling and mood, and our paintings will have much more impact. For example, tonal value can be used to create a sense of space through aerial perspective. In a similar way, bright colours seem to advance and dull colours recede when placed near each other, and this is another way of modelling forms and creating space. Touches of bright colour among areas of duller colour or grey will also attract the viewer's eye and can draw attention to the centre of interest.

THE COLOUR WHEEL

Colours when used together can be either harmonious or contrasting, and the easiest way to understand this is by looking at the colour wheel. Without wishing to bore you, we need to remind ourselves that the colour wheel is made up of primary colours and secondary colours. The primary colours are red, yellow and blue – these colours cannot be mixed from other colours. The secondary colours can be made by mixing pairs of primaries: red and yellow for orange, blue and yellow for green, red and blue for violet. The colour wheel is laid out in such a way that it provides a visual demonstration of this.

A glance at the colour wheel also tells us which colours are harmonious when used together and which are contrasting. Harmonious colours are those close to each other on the wheel – oranges and reds, reds and violets, greens and yellows and so on. Contrasting colours – usually known as complementary colours –

are directly opposite each other: red and green are complementary, as are yellow and violet, and blue and orange. Another way to remember the complementary pairs is that a complementary pair contains all three primaries: red/green (blue and yellow); yellow/violet (red and blue); blue/orange (red and yellow).

USING COMPLEMENTARY COLOURS
You'll find that knowing which colours complement each other will make a huge difference when you're painting because when complementary colours are placed near each other, they immediately appear livelier. For example, if you have a predominantly green scene, you can add a touch of light red and it will really bring the greens alive. As I've said before, there may not be any of the complementary colour in the scene you are looking at, but put in touches of it anyway, whether it's there or not. You'll find this much easier once you know the complementary pairs.

I've used the complementary colours blue and orange to draw attention to the centre of interest, and colours close to blue – violet-blue, blue-green, green and yellow-green – in other areas such as the sky, middle distance and distance, to provide interest without creating distracting contrasts.

WARM AND COOL COLOUR

Another quality of colour that artists use to their advantage is the fact that colours appear to be either warm or cool. The colours on the red side of the wheel – that is, yellows, oranges, browns and reds – are described as warm, and those on the blue side – blues and greens – are described as cool. Warm colours appear to advance when they occur near cool colours; and cool colours seem to recede when they are placed near warm colours. Most colours vary between warm and cool depending on the colours around them as well. A lemon yellow, which has a slight tendency towards green, will appear cool next to something like a cadmium yellow deep, which tends towards orange, but warm beside a blue green, which is very cool.

The warm/cool quality of colours is a very useful and effective way in which we can create a sense of space in a painting and to differentiate between objects that are nearer and those that are further away. This is done by having predominantly warm colours for nearer parts of the scene and cooler colours for things that are more distant.

You can also use warm and cool colours to introduce variety into areas that are predominantly one colour, and predominantly warm or cool colours can be used to create mood in a painting – more of this later.

It's possible to use very subtle warm and cool colours to produce recession. In this scene there is a cool background, with warm colours in the middle distance and foreground. I allowed the colour in the middle distance to blend into the background to create a more subtle contrast.

Here, I've used a strong warm/cool contrast to create a sense of space. The warmest colour – a brown-orange – has been placed in the foreground, establishing this as the nearest part of the scene, with the yellow rock slightly back in space. Against these the blue hills recede into the distance.

A limited range of colours, shown in the swatch, was used to good effect here, showing that you don't always have to use a large number of colours. Warm and cool colours, from orange in the foreground, through warm and cool greens, to blue-green and blue in the distance, contribute to the sense of space in this scene. Purple, which is almost opposite orange on the colour wheel, provides contrast in the foreground. Touches of cooler colours – in this case greens – have been included in the foreground and touches of warmer colour – yellow – around the skyline.

VARIETY

Another way to create interest and excitement in your paintings is to use a variety of colours, even in areas that initially seem to be all one colour, and this is one of the biggest differences between paintings by amateurs and those by professionals. In the beginning the tendency is to think that you must paint exactly what's in front of you – painting a wooden fence flat brown all over, for example – whereas the professional introduces lots of colours into a painting, whether they are there in the subject or not.

Students sometimes ask such questions as – what colour is a stone wall? The answer is that there's every colour in it from purples and browns to pale blue-greys and warm yellow. Even in Venice some painters

Top, I've tried to get a good variety of colours into the snow, water and trees that make up this scene, in order to avoid the monotony that can so easily creep in with this type of subject.

Above, in this stone bridge I've introduced a range of colours from red-brown to blue-grey, through dull yellow and green. The shadows in the arches consist of blue blending into brown. As well as appearing closer than the blue-grey side, the warm left-hand side of the bridge is also shown to be the area receiving most light.

In these buildings I've used a range of warm reds, yellows, greens and cool blues. The road also varies from yellow to blue. None of these surfaces have been painted with single colours, and I've allowed the colours to blend and mix.

treat walls as if they'd been painted with emulsion – with no variety in the colours. Any wall should have lots of colour in it, not just one.

What we have to aim to do as artists is to enhance the subject by introducing variety into the colours we use for each part of the subject, not just take the scene as we find it. For example, you shouldn't paint trees a flat green just because the general impression they give is green. Look carefully and you'll see that trees are made up of a variety of greens from cool, shadowy blue-greens to light, bright yellow-greens, plus other colours such as ochry brown, violet brown or orange, depending on the type of tree and the time of year, and you need to use all these colours in order to make the trees interesting. Ways to handle a variety of colours such as these are covered in the chapter on Gradation.

Another habit we need to break if we're to improve our painting is that of both seeing and using flat, dead greys. Any grey area in your scene, such as a road, will be greatly enhanced by the introduction of browns and blues into your washes. Don't be afraid to use and to experiment with colour. Avoid monotony at all costs!

Another common mistake is to think of greys as just being mixtures of black and white. Try instead to think of this colour in terms of warm and cool greys. There's a whole variety between brown and blue, for example, which you can get just by mixing these colours in different proportions.

This is another reason why it is useful to know about complementary colours. Although complementary colours placed side by side make each other brighter, when mixed together they produce interesting brown/greys, and these can be pushed towards either warm or cool. Blue and orange, for example, will give an orange-brown, which can be warmed up with more orange, or cooled by adding more blue.

Right, here I mixed a range of different greys – dark brown and blue greys for the foreground, lighter blue-grey for the sea, paler green and brown greys for the headland, very cold violet-grey for the distant mountains, with violets and blues in the sky. Although there are no bright colours, it is still a colourful painting.

Below, I painted this with a range of greys, adding a touch of bright red that really sings against the more sombre colours.

A range of different, interesting greys and browns can be made by mixing colours that are complementaries or near complementaries. From the top: **1** *ultramarine + red,* **2** *ultramarine + burnt umber,* **3** *ultramarine + burnt umber but with more burnt umber,* **4** *ultramarine + green,* **5** *raw sienna + ultramarine,* **6** *raw sienna + ultramarine but with more raw sienna,* **7** *ultramarine with a touch of burnt umber,* **8** *ultramarine + light red,* **9** *light red + burnt umber,* **10** *light red + burnt umber but with more light red. Different amounts of water have been added to these mixtures to vary the tonal values of the resulting greys and browns.*

PRACTICE

Look for subjects with large expanses of foliage, or a good-sized area like walls of buildings, and see how much colour you can work into them. This doesn't mean you have to produce rainbow-coloured paintings. Use groups of harmonious colours, or work round the colour wheel from warm to cool across the area you are painting, and try to achieve an even gradation from one colour to another.

CREATING MOOD WITH COLOUR

Mood in a painting is created through the amount of warmth or coolness in the colours you use. Many people make the mistake that I made, the first time I was painting in Spain. My paintings all ended up looking like the Yorkshire Moors because my colours were too cold. I wasn't warming them up enough to create a hot, sunny atmosphere, and now, when I take my own students to a hot climate like Greece, many make the same mistake. They don't see the bouncing light and the warm colours in the shadows, and instead they paint shadows as a slab of cold grey, which creates entirely the wrong feeling.

When thinking about the colours you are going to use, remember that a painting should be predominantly warm or predominantly cool, depending on the mood you want to convey. You wouldn't, for example, paint a snow scene in warm colours. You'd paint it in cool blues, greys and violet, but to emphasize the coldness, you need to include touches of warm colour, such as tree trunks, fallen leaves or dried grasses.

Autumn scenes usually consist of warm, earthy colours – reds, oranges and terracottas – but even then you need to include touches of cool colour to offset and enhance them.

Above, warm bright colours and strong colour contrasts – particularly red and green – portray the sense of a warm, bright day and lots of activity.

Left, in this scene I've used cold colours, mainly greys, with only the merest hints of a warm yellow, to evoke the atmosphere of biting cold on an overcast winter's day.

PRACTICE

Try mixing greys from each of the complementary pairs in turn, painting a graduated scale from one colour to the other, like the ones on page 75. This will help you get to know what type of grey or brown you get from each pair and will give you practice in pushing them towards warm and cool.

Next, try painting a subject using lots of different greys. It is important here to mix the greys from other colours – don't use black and white. Create warm and cool, and light and dark greys by varying the proportions of water to pigment that you use. A good way of drawing attention to a particular area is to add accents of bright colour.

DESIGNING A PAINTING

Line, direction, shape, tonal value, texture and colour are tools that we must use and manipulate to emphasize or play down different features in the composition, depending on what we want to convey about the subject. We must use these tools to produce balanced compositions in which harmonious and varied shapes, tones, textures and colours create visual interest in all parts of the painting, while the principles of contrast and dominance are used to direct the viewer's attention to the most important features, so that they all come together in a unified whole.

Lines and shapes, tones and colours are carefully organized in this painting so that they work together to create a unified and pleasing composition. I developed a strong tonal contrast between the dark boats and the light building in the middle distance to draw attention to the main centre of interest and draw the eye through the scene, while touches of bright red among the greens and green-greys add interest to the foliage and give a feeling of bright sunlight.

Balance

One of the most important aspects of composition is that of balance. If a painting doesn't have a sense of balance, it will look unsatisfactory, no matter what else you do. Unfortunately, nature doesn't present us with nicely balanced scenes, and it's always tempting just to paint a scene without thinking about balance. However, as I've said already, your job as an artist is to manipulate your subject, and this applies to creating balance as to everything else.

Balance is a way of making things look right. It's a matter of arranging features that are different in size, tone, colour, shape and texture so that they balance each other visually. This shouldn't be as difficult as it sounds because most of us have an inbuilt sense of visual balance – we can tell just by looking at something whether it is well balanced or not – yet some people still produce rather unbalanced paintings. This usually happens because they just haven't thought about the balance of the composition before they start painting.

Here again, tonal sketches are invaluable, because they give you a chance to see whether you are achieving a balanced distribution of light, mid and dark tones, and whether the shapes of the main elements in the composition balance each other, before you start working in colour. It takes trial and error to make elements look balanced and the best way to sort this out is in the tonal sketch. You may think that these sketches use up valuable painting time, but they

will save you time, frustration and disappointment in the long run.

You have various options for balancing one feature with another, which I'll go into shortly. First we need to look at the different types of visual balance.

This example has no balance at all because the tree is placed dead centre with nothing in the composition to balance it.

These two features balance each other, but because they are the same size, shape and tone, the effect is dull. Also, they compete with each other for attention.

This is the best example. A larger feature is balanced by a smaller one, creating an asymmetrical sense of balance that is pleasing to look at and avoids boredom.

In the first version of this scene, I've used a large mid-toned tree on the right to balance the main centre of interest – the house and dark tree behind it.

In this version of the scene, I've used the sky to balance the building by developing a large area of darkish cloud towards one corner.

Another option is to add something in the foreground, as I've done in this example, introducing a hedge that is a completely different shape from that of the building.

The small, light-toned shape of the boat's sail is balanced by the much darker-toned mass of rocks and foliage on the left. A quick tonal sketch like the one below helps you to sort out balance before you commit yourself in paint.

The extensive mid-toned shape of the mountain is balanced by the smaller, dark-toned tree, which is curved in shape. Because the tree in the foreground is much darker in tone, it can therefore be much smaller; and, being curved, it sets off the angular shape of the mountain

TYPES OF BALANCE

There are two kinds of balance: formal and informal. You can create a symmetrical composition – which we call formal balance – in which areas that are similar in shape, size, tone, texture or colour are positioned on each side of the picture. They do balance each other, but the effect of this sort of arrangement is dull. This type of picture is also confusing to look at, because if there are two equally important features in a painting, the viewer won't know which part to concentrate on and the eye will keep moving between the two.

A much better way to create balance is by using an asymmetrical composition – or informal balance – and this is much more enjoyable and interesting to look at. You achieve this by balancing one feature with another that has a different shape, size, tonal value and colour.

Left, the warm oranges, reds and browns used to convey the warmth of a summer's day have been balanced by the use of a sharp, cool yellow over the relatively small area of the woman's dress.

Below, the dull, broken colours that convey a damp moorland scene are here balanced by the bright orange of the roof. Because the orange is much brighter than the rest of the colours, it only needs to occupy a small area and still be effective.

SHAPE AND TONE

When trying to balance shapes of different sizes, think of them as a see-saw. A larger person near the centre can be balanced by a smaller one at the edge. Similarly, a large shape near the centre of a painting can be balanced by a smaller one near the edge. Always remember that you can use the sky to balance a picture. If you've got a strong, dark object near one corner, you can balance it with a dark area of sky in the opposite corner.

A dark shape or area gives the impression of being heavier than a light one, so a small dark shape can balance a larger light shape. Think of the shapes in your composition as weights that have to be balanced, and again the best way to work this out is beforehand in the tonal sketch.

COLOUR BALANCE

Colours in a composition, too, must be balanced, and if the colours in your painting are all too bright or too dull, too light or too dark, it will seem unbalanced. Areas of bright colour can be balanced by subdued colours and vice versa, but the brighter the bright colour, the smaller the area it should occupy. Conversely, the more muted the subdued colour, the larger the area it should occupy to achieve a balance between the two.

If your painting has a predominantly warm mood, balance this with a few spots of cool colour; if cool, balance it with some touches of warmth.

In this scene, small dark-toned areas are balanced by large mid-toned areas, the overall cool mood is balanced by touches of warmth in the hedges and undergrowth, small areas of rough texture are balanced by the larger, smooth-textured areas of snow, and the curved shapes of the trees are balanced by the small, hard-edged angular shape of the building.

Harmony

Harmonious elements in a painting are those that are similar, and these are vital to our paintings because they can create interest in less important areas while at the same time unifying the composition. Harmonious colours are those that are close to each other on the colour wheel, such as orange and red (see page 68). Harmonious shapes are similar – a circle and an oval for example, or a square and a rectangle – and harmonious sizes are those which are close together. Straight and slightly curved lines are harmonious, as are close tonal values. In short, harmony is the opposite of contrast.

Unlike contrast, harmony involves subtle, gentle changes that you can use to introduce interest into a subject that would otherwise be dull, without changing things completely. For example, imagine you're painting a row of rocks that are all the same shape. Don't paint them all the same just because that's the way they are. You need to find ways to change them by slightly varying their shapes and sizes. Or if you've got a row of fence posts in your painting, don't make them all upright and equally spaced.

Instead, vary the distances between them a little, and paint one or two at different angles. You don't need to make them very different – just a little different, to avoid boredom.

When you're painting distant mountains, you can change one mountain by making it just a little bit more mauve, while another mountain can be painted with more blue; this technique gives a touch of variety yet still keeps both mountains in the distance.

Of course, you can also use harmony to bring very different shapes or colours closer together if you need to unify the composition or to play down a supporting feature. Contrasts in tone, texture, shape, size, colour and so on can be reduced in less important areas of a painting in order to help concentrate attention on the main focus of interest.

One of the best ways to create harmony throughout a painting is to use a very limited number of colours – say, three that represent the three primaries in some form – and to mix all the other colours you need from those three. This will give you a wide range of colours but a very unified effect.

I've introduced harmonious interest into the sky area by repeating circular shapes in the clouds that occur in the landscape and the main tree. Other trees and bushes in the hedgerows are also curved, and I've even softened the outline of the distant mountain to give the painting a sense of unity.

I've varied the textures in the foreground in a subtle way while keeping them harmonious in order to create interest there without introducing a strong contrast.

The differences in tonal values have been minimized, an harmonious range of colours has been used and variations in texture have been kept to a minimum in order to create a tranquil and unified scene.

This has been painted with a limited range of colours – mainly orange, red, purple-red and purple – with small touches of blue. In areas such as the ground in front of the cottage, and the hillside on the left, a variety of colours has been used, but because they are harmonious they are not distracting.

Interest has been added to the land and sky with a series of curving lines. I have varied the amount of curve very gently across the scene so that it does not dominate the composition.

COLOUR HARMONY

You can introduce interest into areas that are all one colour by adding touches of harmonious colour, ie, colours on either side of the main colour on the colour wheel (see page 68). For example, if you are doing an area of grass, instead of painting it all one green, add in touches of blue-green, which will keep it cool and also provide interest.

If you are painting a scene in predominantly warm or cool colours and want to add touches of the opposite without creating a strong contrast, you need to choose a colour that is harmonious with the predominant colours. An example of this is a moorland scene painted in predominantly cool blues and violets. You would not want to add in touches of bright yellow or

orange, as these would create an unwanted contrast of complementary colours. In this situation, you should choose colours that are closer on the colour wheel to the dominant colour – in this example, the colours to select would be yellow-green and red-purple.

Above, straight and slightly curving lines, similar in direction, mainly rough, hard textures, and a limited range of predominantly cool colours have been used to produce an harmonious, unified composition that describes the bright, harsh light of winter sunshine.

Above left, predominantly cool, harmonious colours have been used: blues, blue-green and greens with touches of yellow, which is close to green, to add interest without contrast. These closely related colours, shown in the swatch, convey an atmosphere of tranquillity. The light on the water and in the foliage has been created by leaving the paper white.

PRACTICE

In order to get to know groups of harmonious colours, choose a scene with a predominant mood – warm and bright, or cold and frosty – or at a particular time of day, and paint it using a group of three harmonious colours that convey the mood. You can use light and dark and bright and dull versions of the colours you choose, so try experimenting with different variations on these three colours. Then choose a different scene and a different group of colours.

Select an old painting and do a new version introducing subtle, harmonious changes.

Gradation

Gradation is the tool to add interest and variety in an area, large or small, without drawing attention to it through an abrupt contrast. Yet because gradation isn't always obvious in nature, many amateur painters don't think about it when they are painting. They see green grass or a brown shed and that's how they paint it – all one colour. But if all areas of a painting are done with washes of flat colour, the result is dull. Gradation also applies to the other elements of a painting, too, such as shape and texture.

So, to create interesting paintings, we have to use gradation, which basically means creating a gradual change – from a warm colour to a cool one, or from a light tone to a dark one, from one type of line to another or one size or type of shape to another. Tonal and colour gradation are particularly useful for large empty areas, such as a sky or foreground, because they enable you to add interest in these areas without having to put in anything specific that would detract from your overall composition.

Gradation can also help to increase the sense of distance and space in a painting. By gradually decreasing the size of objects as they recede into the horizon, and by gradually reducing the tonal contrast, you can create the perception that the scene recedes into the distance.

Gradation is something that you have to do for yourself; as I've said, it isn't always apparent in nature. So next time, remember that you may have to cheat a little to make it exciting. It is worth studying the work of professional painters to see the gradations in colour and tone that they achieve.

COLOUR

Colours can be gradated in different ways: from warm to cool, from one colour to its complementary, or from bright to dull. When going from a warm colour to a cool one, work through the colours in between them on the colour wheel. For example, on a

Gradual changes in colour from warm to cool and light to dark, and in the shapes, from those of the mountains in the distance to the hillocks in the foreground, even the textures from rough to smooth across the foreground, have all been introduced to create interest in all parts of the painting while the number and placement of eye-catching contrasts has been controlled.

fence you can go from warm brown, through red and violet to cool blue. When working from a colour to its complementary, do so via the grey/browns in between that you obtain by mixing the two. This creates a contrast, but in a gradual way. Because it's not eye-catching it's something we can use a lot, whereas sudden contrasts need to be used with discretion to direct attention to the main areas of interest.

Imagine you are painting an area of grass. Most people would paint it a flat, monochrome green, even if it extends back a long way. This is an example where the professional artist would cool down the green a little in the distance by adding a touch more blue, and warm it up along the nearer edge, possibly by adding a little raw sienna. The area is still green, but it has gradually been varied to create a feeling of distance.

TONE

Just as areas of flat colour look dull and unnatural, so the same effect is created by areas of flat tone. Although earlier I talked about massing tones together in order to simplify your subject and exclude unwanted detail, you still need to introduce gradations in tonal value in all areas of your paintings to make them interesting to the viewer.

The other important aspect about gradated tone is that we can use it to model a rounded form, and to help create a sense of space. Closely gradated tones across a surface will make it appear gently curved, whereas a sharp contrast will create an abrupt change of plane. A gradual reduction in tonal contrast towards the distance in a scene will help to create a feeling of receding space (see Aerial perspective, page 56).

Left, texture has been gradually changed from rough to smooth and the sizes of individual shapes have been gradually reduced back through the scene in order to create a sense of depth.

Above, colours have been gradated from warm to cool and tones from dark to light from foreground to distance – in the sky as well as the landscape – to produce a strong sense of space.

SHAPE AND SIZE

Gradation can be applied to shape and size. If you were painting a row of rocks, for example, that were all the same shape, you could gradually change the shape from rounded at one end of the row to angular at the other end. You could also make them gradually larger or smaller.

TEXTURE

Textural effects can gradually be reduced from foreground to background. Greater texture is apparent in the foreground than in the distance, so if you gradually reduce a textural effect, this will have the effect of increasing the feeling of distance.

Here, I've given interest to the foreground areas through gradual changes in tone and from warm to cool colours, moving from orange-brown to grey-blue; I've worked a variety of colours into the road as well. The same colours have been used from foreground to background.

Above, this scene moves from warm orange-browns in the foreground through green to blue-grey in the distance, creating a gradual but strong sense of recession.

Left, the water and rocks have a variety of colours. These are things that people are often tempted to paint as a flat colour. Here you can see how it's possible to play warms and cools and lights and darks against each other by gradually moving between them, which gives you a varied but continuous surface.

Contrast

Whereas we use gradation to avoid boredom in the less important areas of a painting, we can use contrast to generate excitement and interest and to focus attention on the main subject. Contrast is created by placing opposites next to each other: a light next to a dark tone, a warm colour against a cool one, a large shape next to a small one or a rounded shape next to an angular one, horizontal lines next to vertical ones and so on. For example, if you want to emphasize a white building in a painting, no matter how small the building is, you can do this by placing a dark tree or some other dark shape behind it. And as strong contrasts seldom occur where you need them, you would probably need to invent or exaggerate this dark shape in order to create the contrast.

Strong contrasts have to be placed deliberately and carefully in a painting by the artist, by inventing or exaggerating certain features, because they seldom occur naturally. The strong tonal contrasts in hot countries are an obvious exception to this.

Although contrast is the element that creates excitement, it shouldn't be over-used or the painting will become too busy and confusing to look at. As contrasts attract the eye, use them where you want to focus the viewer's attention.

PRACTICE

Look at paintings by the old masters to study the high degree of tonal organization in their work and the way they used strong contrasts between light and shadow. You can make small monochrome studies from their work, which will help you understand the way they have used tonal contrasts. Aim to match the same intensity of contrast in your studies that they achieved. Rembrandt and Goya are good artists to study for this technique as they both used effects of light and shade to great dramatic effect in their work.

Look through your old paintings and pull out a few that look weak and flat. Think about the ways in which you could increase either the tonal or colour contrasts in them to create more interest and focus. Then work over them again, or repaint them, to see how far you need to push the tonal and colour contrasts in order to make the paintings stronger. Really deepen your dark colours and experiment with extremes of light and dark, but ensure you use one over a larger area than the other.

The square shape of the pier is contrasted with the curved shapes of the boats, which immediately draws attention to this part of the painting.

A horizontal against a vertical contrast, as seen here in the trees and their shadows, and the overall direction of the building, creates a strong, stable composition. The wooden fence echoes this structure.

Left, hard and soft textures are set against each other here, creating visual interest and liveliness.

Below, light and dark shapes placed next to each other draw the eye to the boat and on to the building. Contrasts can be used in this way to lead the eye around the picture.

This is based on a contrast of complementary colours – yellow against purple – which draw attention to the lemon, and also create a lively, light-filled picture.

The attention is drawn to the little boat through the large contrast in size between it and the overwhelming surroundings.

TONAL CONTRAST

I make no apology for repeating myself in saying that tonal contrast is the most important element in creating an interesting painting, and you need to use a wide range of tones, so that you've got light enough lights and dark enough darks to create good contrast.

The deliberate placing of light against dark is called counterchange, and you'll need to exaggerate what you see in order to create it because counterchange doesn't always occur in nature, or not where you want it. When looking at a scene, you've got to see where you can achieve that really strong contrast. As I've said before, it's no good just sitting there painting what you see – you must deliberately intensify what is there in order to get clarity.

You need to play lighter and darker tones against each other in other parts of the painting as well in order to make other elements in the scene clear. For example, if there is a telegraph pole beside a road, with the bottom half seen against foliage and the top half against the sky, you need to make the lower part of the pole lighter than the foliage and the top part darker than the sky so that it shows up against both of them.

Counterchange has been used here to make sense of all the different forms in the composition. Lights and darks have been played against each other to define figures, umbrellas, trees and so on. The strong contrasts distributed through the scene also convey a sense of activity and bright sunshine.

PRACTICE

When you are out and about, look for examples of contrasts, or potential contrasts, all around you and make notes in a sketchbook. These could be things like a large tree with a small letter-box or gate below it; the rounded foliage of a bush against the angular shape of a building; a dark shape silhouetted against a bright light; a rough-textured object against a soft one. As you do these sketches, make any adjustments to the objects or shapes themselves, or their positions, that are needed in order to create the maximum contrast between them. Such sketches may provide the basis for more considered paintings.

Left, a more subtle use of counterchange, where alternation between light and mid tones is used to produce the effect of the broken surface of the water. The tree trunk to the left has been picked out by deliberately making it lighter in tone than the background.

Right, strong colour contrasts between complementaries can create a vibrancy that almost matches that created by a strong tonal contrast. Here I've used yellow and purple to create a powerful and compelling image where your attention is immediately drawn to the flowers. All other areas of the painting have been subordinated to this effect through a reduction in colour and tonal contrasts.

Below, you need to look for opportunities to create contrast where there isn't any. In this woodland scene I introduced a pheasant with curving shapes to contrast with the large, in effect, rectangular shape of the tree trunk. I placed the bird, which is dark in tone, against white snow to emphasize the contrast.

Right, the tonal contrast between the white walls and the dark roof of the cottage is surrounded by areas where the changes in tone are gradual. Strong warm/cool colour contrasts among the boats – especially between blue and orange – add interest and a good sense of light and shadow, whereas in the sand, the changes from warm to cool are more gradual.

You need to be continually re-assessing the strength of the tonal contrasts in all parts of your painting as you work. Keep the strongest contrast for the centre of interest, with less contrast in other areas so as not to detract from it. These contrasts are important because, as they attract the eye, they create a sense of movement and help the viewer to explore the painting. You can also use them to describe the effect of light by using strong sunlight against deep shadow. However, use this effect with subtlety.

COLOUR CONTRASTS

As I've explained already, complementary pairs form a contrast, as do warm and cool colours (see page 68-71). Also, each complementary pair of colours forms a warm/cool contrast as well – which is quite useful. Although neither warm nor cool colours should dominate in a painting, you need to include touches of a contrasting colour to bring out the qualities of the dominant colour. An area of duller colours can be brought alive by touches of bright colour nearby.

An effective way to create mood through colour and to introduce contrast is to choose a group of three harmonious colours, as we did in the practice session in the previous chapter, and the complementary of the middle one of those three colours – you'll need to refer back to the colour wheel for this (page 68). As an example: you might choose to paint a scene in yellow, yellow-greens and greens, in which case you would use touches of violet-red – the complementary of yellow-green – for contrast.

SHAPE AND SIZE
An abrupt change from an angular shape to a curved one creates a strong contrast, as does a tiny shape placed next to a large one. Any type of strong contrast will catch the viewer's interest and form the most exciting part of a picture.

Variation

Imagine you are painting a row of poplars or telegraph poles. Would you paint them all the same size and colour, all equally spaced apart and at the same angle? If you did, you would produce a rather dull painting. As an artist, you have got to make all aspects of your subject interesting to look at, whether they are or not, and a way of doing this is to introduce as much variation as you possibly can in all areas of your paintings.

Variation is a form of repetition, but it is repetition with change – whether an abrupt change (contrast), a gradual change (gradation), or a slight change (harmony). You can vary the types and directions of lines and shapes, the tonal values and colours in each part of the painting, and the textures.

With the row of poplars, make some large and some small, include different kinds of trees as well, vary the distances between them, and their colours, and make one or two grow at an angle. If you must paint a row of telegraph poles, vary the distance between them, make them different heights and put some at an angle. Don't

be carried away by what you see. It's up to you to make these changes in order to add variety and interest to your paintings.

You need to consider all areas and aspects of your painting when you are thinking about variation. If you are including two buildings, for instance, they should vary in shape, size and proportion, but you also need to check that they are different distances from the sides of the painting. You need to make sure that elements in different parts of a scene, such as clouds and foliage, don't repeat each other too closely in terms of size, shape and tonal value, even if they are very similar in reality. Alter one of them if they are becoming repetitious in your painting.

Another, more subtle aspect of repetition can occur when the dimensions of features such as a building, the distances between it and the edges of the painting, or the depth of the foreground or the sky, are similar. This can happen accidentally and it is something you need to guard against. Again, if necessary, make adjustments to the positioning of features when you

Left, similar clumps of rock have been varied in shape and size so that they don't become monotonous. The variation in tone gives a sense of near and far rocks, emphasized by the touches of warm colour on the ones closest.

Two trees have been included but the shapes and directions of growth has been varied. Also notice that I've positioned the two trees on the diagonal in relation to each other, which creates a more unified effect than if they are placed side by side.

Top, in this version of the scene I've introduced variation in colour, and through direction and brushstrokes. I've used strong directional brushstrokes that vary in direction along the bank of the river. The colours in the foliage are varied from blue to yellow-green to add interest, and I've varied the colours in the castle walls from cool greys to warm yellow-greens.

Above, I've used counterchange here to silhouette the shape of the castle, creating a dramatic effect. In other parts of the painting I've gradated the tones to give interest without detracting from the impact of the castle itself, set against the background foliage and dark sky.

In this scene I've created variation in tone through all parts of the composition. Similarly, I've introduced variation in colour into the water, foliage and the stone walls of the castle and the shapes of trees around the castle and in the background so that they are not monotonous.

plan the composition to avoid this. A similar form of repetition can occur when you have a road or stream zigzagging through a scene. The angle and length of each part of the zigzag should vary or your painting will look stilted and unnatural.

You need to introduce variation within quite small areas as well as across a whole painting. Even quite small patches of colour or tone should vary, either through gradation from lighter to darker or warmer to cooler, or through slight, subtle, more harmonious changes. Similarly, small variations should occur in areas of texture, even around the edges of objects. If you study the paintings of professional watercolourists, you'll notice that hard-edged objects are not painted with a hard edge all the way round, but the edge will have been softened in one or two places.

Dominance

Dominance is the most important aspect of designing a painting and we need to think about it in relation to all aspects – shape, line, direction, texture, edge qualities, tonal values and colour. It is vital because it makes clear what is most important in any painting. Of all the different types of shapes in your painting, one should be dominant; of the different types of lines, one should be dominant; there should be a dominant direction, a dominant tone, a dominant colour mood and a dominant texture. Although it might sound rather daunting to apply this principle to all the elements in every painting: it really is important to try to apply it to as many elements as possible.

One kind of dominance that should always be apparent in your work is dominance of subject, and this goes back to what I said earlier on the importance

Dominance can be created in a variety of ways.

Top left, this shows dominance through colour – the foreground boat is dominant because it is a much brighter colour than the other boats.

Bottom left, I've created a directional dominance here through the much greater incidence of vertical lines compared to diagonal or horizontal ones.

Right, this scene has a strong horizontal dominance, this sense of direction being created through line and shape.

Below, smooth textures dominate in the roses and the vase – compared to the spikier texture of the foliage – and coincide with the dominant rounded shapes.

of being clear in your own mind about your centre of interest. If you are painting a boating scene, for example, you must select one boat and make it larger and more dominant than the rest. If the scene in front of you doesn't possess a dominant feature, you must create one. And having selected your dominant feature, you can then use dominance of line, shape, tone, texture or colour to support it.

CREATING DOMINANCE

There are various ways of making a certain type of line, shape, tone, texture or colour the dominant one. You can have more of one thing than the others. For example, of the different types of shape – rounded, angular and squarish – make one type occur more often than the rest. You can make one type of line – straight or curved – occur more often than the other,

Left, this painting has a definite angular dominance, which I've developed through repeating angular shapes several times throughout the foreground and distance, although I've taken care to vary them.

Below, I've used oblique lines more than vertical or horizontal ones in order to create dominance of direction, and I've used a bright red on the roof, which is intensified by the surrounding green foliage, to create colour dominance and draw attention to the buildings.

and one direction. The same applies to other elements of a painting, such as tones, textures and colours.

You can make one shape, or area of tone or colour larger than the rest. This shape will then be dominant in a painting, but the difference in size must be such that it appears larger even when the painting is seen from a distance. To make mid-tones dominant, they should cover a larger area than the light or dark tones.

The same applies to colour – to create a dominant warm mood, use warm colours over a much larger area of the painting than cool colours, and vice versa.

Another way to make something dominant is to make it brighter than other parts of the painting. If shapes of a similar size are subdued in colour, a bright shape will appear dominant because it is more easily seen. The same applies to line and texture.

COLOUR

As I have just explained, to produce a predominantly warm or cool mood, the warm or cool colours should cover a larger area than the others. However, not all warm colours are equally warm. Red-orange is much warmer than yellow-green. If your warm painting is not turning out very warm because you're using the cooler warms, add a touch of a very warm colour to emphasize the warm dominance. The same applies if you are using cool colours.

The test of whether you have been successful is to ask someone to look at your painting. If they are in no doubt about what the subject is, whether the work has a warm or cool mood, or is predominantly light or dark in tone, whether the textural quality of the subject is rough, hard or soft, and what is the main directional thrust of the composition, then you have achieved your aim!

PRACTICE

Look through your old paintings and ask yourself what is the main subject of each, what is the dominant mood, tonal value, texture and direction. If you can't answer these questions, think about ways in which you could create dominance in these different aspects. Try re-working some of your old paintings, creating dominance in one or two aspects of each.

Select a scene to paint, and before starting even a sketch, consider what aspects or qualities you particularly want to emphasize through dominance. You might want to jot them down to serve as a reminder as you develop a painting.

Then make a second painting of the same scene, altering the emphasis by playing down features that were dominant in the first painting, and making something else dominant instead.

Several kinds of dominance have been created in this painting. Predominantly warm colours have been used to evoke a sunny day, and dominance of direction has been created through the repetition of diagonal lines, evoking the tangled appearance of a wood.

Above, a strong vertical dominance is created here through linear elements and vertical shapes with the buildings, and a cool colour dominance has been produced through the use of violets, blues and cool crimson.

Right, the very light tone of the bridge ensures that it dominates this scene. Dominance of shape is achieved through the repeated use of a variety of curved shapes – in the bridge, the foliage and the line of the hills in the distance.

Unity

A painting must be a complete unit, not a collection of bits and pieces. It doesn't matter if you are the best painter in the world, from a technical point of view, if your picture doesn't hang together as a unit, you'll never make it. I see so many examples of students' work which contain all the necessary elements – trees, buildings, a river – but these are scattered like bits of broken glass across the picture because they don't know how to lock them together into a unified whole.

Be careful not to put one type of line, shape, texture, tone or colour in only one part of the painting, because this gives a fragmented impression. To unify a painting, elements – shapes, colours, textures and so on – should be repeated, or echoed, in all areas. This links different parts of the painting together visually. A large foreground tree can be echoed by a small distant tree; a cloud shape could be repeated in a foreground bush; a large building could be echoed by a distant building.

The positioning of these repeats is important. Place a repeat or echo of a shape or colour in another part of the painting and on the diagonal to the first if possible, because then they balance each other in an asymmetrical way. Avoid putting them side by side, on a level with each other if possible, and never place one above or below the other, because this looks unbalanced and very unnatural. Also remember to apply the other principles – variation, gradation, harmony, dominance, contrast etc – to repeated shapes, colours and tones.

One of the important and effective ways to create a unified painting is by linking shapes together. Your tonal sketches, or the simplified monochrome sketch we did in the chapter on Balance (page 80) will help you see whether the shapes in your composition link up well. When assessing a sketch before starting to paint, ask yourself whether the dark shapes link up

Right, calligraphic brushmarks, used for the grasses and leafless trees, have been repeated throughout the picture to link together different areas of the composition.

Left, linear elements have been distributed throughout the composition, with the strong vertical emphasis of the foreground trees being echoed in the background.

The warm colours of the foreground have been echoed in the sky, and the blue-purple in the sky is reflected in the water, unifying the composition through echoed colours.

The strong angular shapes of the rocks in the foreground are echoed by the hills in the distance, visually linking the two parts of the painting.

with each other, likewise the light shapes. If they don't, your painting will look disjointed and bitty. Adjust the tones of different elements in the composition so that dark and light areas are linked. This doesn't mean they actually have to join up with each other, but they need to be close enough to be linked visually.

Another aspect of linking shapes is to make sure you have interlocking pieces in the painting. I always encourage my students to think about this. Look at the positive and negative shapes in your painting, and make sure that they lock in to each other, like the pieces of a jigsaw puzzle. If your light and dark shapes are linking up well, this should give you good interlocking shapes.

WHEN IS A PAINTING FINISHED?

A question that bothers many inexperienced artists is when to stop working on a painting. There is no obvious point at which a painting can be described as finished, although there are certain pointers. Usually you reach a stage when you realize that you have got down the main things that you wanted in a painting and you start to fiddle with small details; this is usually the moment to stop – or at least to take a good break so that you can assess your work with a fresh eye. We all have to resist the temptation to go on working for too long on parts of a painting that we're not happy with, because once a painting becomes overworked it loses all vitality and sensitivity and looks muddied and stilted. It is better to stop before you reach this point,

even if it means leaving things that you're not entirely satisfied with. You never know; when you look at the painting again later, you may feel differently about it.

PUTTING IT ALL TOGETHER

It obviously takes time and practice to become proficient at balancing lines and shapes, judging tonal values, painting different textures, creating gradation and harmony, contrast and unity all at once – it seems like a juggling act at first. Don't expect to get every aspect of every element working well in every painting. At first, just concentrate on balance, dominance and unity. Then gradually work on the others, and you'll be surprised at how much they help you to perfect your watercolours.

PRACTICE

Make some sketches of local scenes, concentrating on finding ways to work in smaller repeats and echoes of the main feature in other parts of the composition. Remember as you do this to position the repeats carefully in relation to each other and to introduce variation into them.

Now make monochrome sketches of the same scenes, blocking in the light and dark areas. If these don't link up well in your sketches, try again, making adjustments to tones and shapes until they do.

Left, the shapes of buildings and trees are woven together in order to unify the composition, and the reflections in the foreground also contribute to this effect.

From foreground to background, the shapes of the hills, water and sky interlock to create a unified picture.

This predominantly warm scene, with emphasis falling on the small shape of the fisherman, shows the extent to which you can manipulate the elements in a painting in order to create a striking, varied and unified whole. Notice the dominance of rough textures in the riverbank and the broken water, with counterchange defining different forms against their backgrounds, and a strong sense of recession achieved through the use of aerial perspective.

Index

Acknowledgements

I would like to express my grateful thanks to Ann Mills, who has helped me enormously with the writing and Jenny Hickey who did all the typing from my almost indecipherable scribblings

The publishers would like to thank Cowling & Wilcox Ltd, 26–28 Broadwick Street, London W1V 1FG for supplying the art materials on pages 16–19 and Pro Arte, Sutton-in-Craven, Nr. Keighley, West Yorkshire BD20 7AX for the brushes on page 17.

LIST OF SUPPLIERS

Beaver Art & Framing Ltd,
Monk Street, Monmouth,
Gwent NP5 3NZ.
(Worldwide mail order service)

Berol Ltd,
Oldmedow Road,
King's Lynn,
Norfolk PE30 4JR.
(Worldwide mail order service)

Daler-Rowney Ltd,
PO Box 10,
Bracknell,
Berkshire RG12 8ST.

Daler-Rowney Ltd (USA),
1085 Cranbury South River Road,
Demsburg,
New Jersey 08831,
USA.

Frisk Products Ltd,
7-1 Franthorne Way,
Randlesdown Road,
London SE6 3BT.

Frisk Products (USA) Inc.,
5240 Snapfinger Park Drive,
Suite 115,
Decatur,
Georgia 30035,
USA.

Frisk Products
operate an export service:
Clam Export Ltd,
48 Parsons Mead,
West Croydon,
CR0 3SL.

Pro Arte,
Sutton-in-Craven,
Nr. Keighley,
West Yorkshire BD20 7AX.

Pro Arte (USA),
PO Box 1043,
Big Timber,
Montana 59011,
USA.

Rexel Ltd,
Gatehouse Road,
Aylesbury,
Bucks HP19 3DT.
(and export)

Winsor & Newton,
Whitefriars Avenue,
Wealdstone,
Harrow,
Middlesex HA3 5RH.
(and export)